Do Vegetarians Eat Animal Crackers?
And Other Questions You Might Not
Think To Ask!

By Robert Bimler

© 2008 Robert Bimler

All rights reserved. No part of this publication may be reproduced, stored in a retrieval system, or transmitted in any form by any means, electronic, mechanical, photocopying, or otherwise, without the prior written permission of the publisher, Lulu, Inc.

Printed in the United States of America

ISBN: 978-0-557-02206-9

Sketches: Carrie Idol

Photos, Additional Material: Hal Gieseking

Table Of Contents

Foreword	4
Thoughts From The Author	5
Chapter 1 – Odd Observations	6
Chapter 2 – Animal Antics	31
Chapter 3 – Food For Fun	39
Chapter 4 – Cliché Quandaries	46
Chapter 5 – Insect Insights	52
Chapter 6 – Puns To Ponder	55
Chapter 7 – Word Wisdom	71
Chapter 8 – Human Habits	76
Chapter 9 – Inanimate Issues	81
Another Book To Enjoy!	87
About The Author	88
Reviews	89

FOREWORD

Several years ago I interviewed Bill Moyers, asking him for his definition of creativity. He said, "Creativity is looking at the familiar and seeing the strange. Or looking at the strange and seeing the familiar. It means piercing what we usually take for granted – piercing what is obvious and mundane to find what is marvelous. Creativity is seeing the marvelous in the ordinary, and the ordinary in the marvelous."

I thought about that when I first read Robert Bimler's manuscript. I felt he had found new ways to twist different meanings into obvious clichés and pump new life into puns. I believe these phrases and questions are ideal content that can add fresh style and interest to sleepy e-mails and blogs.

But I also realized that something deeper was going on. Most of Bob's phrases were based on "what if?" thinking. – the keystone words of all creativity from Archimedes and Thomas Edison to Bill Gates. Business and academia today are crying out for more "original thinking" and looking for employees and students who can think creatively. If you can look at a problem and say "what if?" - the new combinations of words and ideas could put you on the road to a solution.

Why not ask yourself a question and begin your journey?

Hal Gieseking
Former Consumer Editor, Travel Holiday magazine and past Travel Consultant for CBS Morning News

Thoughts From The Author

"Should Vegetarians Eat Animal Crackers?" is the culmination of nearly 20 years worth of my observations of human behavior and use of the English language. Inspired by several stand-up comedians, (are there any that sit-down?), I found myself constantly looking at ordinary things in an extraordinary way. I started writing down these thoughts and couldn't stop! This book contains over 1,000 thought provoking questions. Hopefully you will like it so much that once you put it down you won't want to pick it up again!?

The questions and quips inside will give you all kinds of material to use in various activities. You could use them in emails, blogs, and term papers, for business presentations or speaking at corporate outings. The book could also be used like a starter kit for the inexperienced speaker as well as solid material for the seasoned speaker or comedian to add moments of lightness to keep your audience listening. Or you could just read it because it's funny and laughing is healthy!

I hope these quirky questions can be useful to you and will inspire you to look at the world with inquisitive eyes in a fun and creative way!

Robert Bimler

Chapter 1 – Odd Observations

- Why do 7-11's have locks on their doors when they're open 24 hours a day?
- If there was powdered water, what would you add?
- Do you mow your lawn or cut your grass?
- Why do you pay a toll on a freeway?
- Is it bad luck to be superstitious?
- Would you give up your left arm to be ambidextrous?
- When you choke a smurf, what color does it turn?
- Is there a Mrs. Sandman?
- What if Noah's favorite number was five?
- Ever wonder what auctioneers are like at home?
- Is the warning "Do not look for a gas leak with a lighted match" really necessary?
- Has anyone actually seen the movie "Closed For The Season"?
- Is it necessary to brush your teeth during a fast?
- Have you ever experienced amnesia and deja vu at the same time?
- What is the speed of dark?
- Why do we drive on a parkway and park on a driveway?

- Have you ever dreamt you had insomnia?

- If you dig a hole in the South Pole, are you digging up or down?

- What's the opposite of a live band?

- If the universe keeps expanding, then what's on the other side?

- Did the early settlers go camping?

- Why do "Happy Hours" last longer than 60 minutes?

- Do police sketch artists start out by drawing chalk outlines?

- What do people in the Far East call a location to the east of them?

- Has anyone ever been underwhelmed?

- If you wear a sheet for Halloween are you a ghost or a mattress?

- How many "First" Baptists churches are there?

- If a chronic liar tells you he is a chronic liar, do you believe him?

- Are time and temperature readings at banks ever correct?

- How do people who drive snowplows get to work?

- Can you cry under water?

- Why does the last page of a book need to be blank?

- Why do pro tennis players have to grunt every time they hit the ball?

**You can't have <u>everything</u>.
Where would you put it?**

- Why is it that famous people are always born on holidays?

- How does a person know if they've had amnesia?

- Why do country and western radio stations come in the best when you're traveling on the road?

- Can race car drivers deduct speeding tickets?

- Why is it that when you watch a TV show you haven't seen in a while, it's usually an episode you've already seen?

- Now that Microsoft is so big, should it be called Macrosoft?

- Why does hair look shorter the day after you get it cut?

- Is it legal to name a child "Anonymous"?

- What's the difference between a tad, a bit, and a smidgeon?

- Why can't you tickle yourself (but others can)?

- Can only athletes' get athletes' foot?

- If a vampire can't see its reflection, how is their hair always so neat?

- How can one size fit all?

- Why isn't there a special name for the tops or your feet?

- Who was in the kitchen with Dinah?

- Can people who don't have children buy products that come in "family packs"?

- Where do you tell people in hell to go?

- What should you say to God when he sneezes?

- Why do restaurants that have free refills, sell drinks in small, medium, and large sizes?

- Who is this Susan person and how did she get to be so lazy?

- Can you tell how old a pirate is by cutting off his peg leg and counting the rings?

- Why do they put pictures of criminals up in the Post Office? Are we supposed to write to them?

- How can Wile E. Coyote afford all those Acme contraptions and not have any money to buy food?

- Why don't hair permanents last forever?
- Do people who get tickets for going under the speed limit have to go to offensive driving school?
- Why aren't there any coffee length dresses?
- Do people in Australia call the rest of the world "up over"?
- If a person owns a piece of land do they own it all the way down to the core of the earth?
- Don't change machine companies usually break even?
- How can there be "self-help groups"?

Before television did people eat frozen radio dinners?

- What should you do if you step on a tetanus shot needle?
- Why is it called rush hour when nobody's moving?
- What is occasional irregularity?
- Why is easy listening music so hard to listen to?

- Once you're in heaven, do you get stuck wearing the clothes you were buried in for eternity?

- Why is it called Alcoholics Anonymous if the first thing people do is tell their name?

- Would Midol help a man with a leg cramp?

- What do people in China call their good plates?

- Why are there no sit-down comics?

- How come wrong numbers are never busy?

- Why don't angry people ever yell "mice"?

- How did Humpty Dumpty get up on the wall in the first place?

- Where do they get spring water in the other 3 seasons?

- Why don't we say "Father Nature"?

- Has anyone ever gotten seasick on a waterbed?

- How many illegal secretaries are there?

- How is it that we put man on the moon before we figured out it would be a good idea to put wheels on luggage?

- What does Geronimo say when he jumps out of a plane?

- If hell froze over, what would all those people do who promised to perform certain tasks?

- Why isn't there a structure called a dog walk?

- Shouldn't our national park mascot be called "Non-Smokey the Bear"?

- Do you think you'll ever get into the Optimist's Club?
- Why don't we say "Father Earth"?
- How do musicians come up with titles for songs that have no words?
- If Superman is so smart why does he wear his underwear over his pants?
- How can you look up a word in the dictionary if you don't know how to spell it?
- Why isn't there a catwood tree?
- What is the deal with daylight savings time – why are they saving it and where do they keep it?
- Since there is a speed of light and a speed of sound, is there a speed of smell?
- What happened to the first 6 UP's?
- Is a halfback more valuable than a quarterback?
- Wouldn't an auto loan be money you borrow from yourself?
- Why don't they just make food stamps edible?
- Isn't having the word "Ram" on the back of a truck just asking for trouble?
- Has anyone ever just asked for trouble?
- Do people who get jay-walking tickets have to go to walking school?
- If a trailer carrying new cars on it got a speeding ticket, would all the cars get tickets too?

- What would you call the late work shift at a graveyard?
- Have you ever experienced deja vu?
- Why don't weather forecasters ever give us the probability of acid rain?
- Have you ever experienced deja vu?
- Why is there no "Bill of Lefts"?
- Does Allen Capella or A. Capella have to stay single?
- Why don't people say "Mother Time"?
- What did a famous Greek Warrior call the sore tendon at the back of his ankle?
- Who is this guy Cliff, and why can't he read an entire book instead of just taking notes?
- Couldn't you just read your procrastination literature tomorrow?
- Doesn't everyone know what patronizing is?
- Why is it when a door is open it's ajar, but when a jar is open it's not adoor?
- There are windsocks; why aren't there any windshoes?
- Who exactly are THEY and why do THEY know so much?
- Why is the packaging on new DVD's and CD's so hard to open?
- What is a "free" gift? Aren't all gifts free?
- If you didn't get caught, did you really do it?

Don't you wish the mute button on remote controls would work on people and cell phones in movie theaters!

- How can someone be awfully cute?

- Isn't every place within walking distance if you have the time?

- Why don't you ever hear about racquetball size hail?

- How can singers who can't speak English very well sing very clear English?

- Do really big sports fans that have psychic powers have ESPN?

- What is Victoria's secret?

- Who is this guy "Surge" that everyone is protecting themselves from?

- Why is South Bend in Northern Indiana?

- Do you really care what apathetic means?

- Has anyone actually bought a sidewalk or garage at a sale?

- Why can a woman buy a pair of pants but only one bra?
- How do you know how much an item is worth if it is priceless?
- Why don't restaurants offer kitty bags?
- Where does the fire go when the fire goes out?
- Why do you need a driver's license to buy liquor when you can't drink and drive?
- What happens if you go on a survival course and you don't pass?
- Why are cigarettes sold in gas stations when smoking is prohibited?
- Do you need a silencer if you are going to shoot a mime?
- Why do they put Braille dots on the key pad of the drive-up ATM?
- Are you breaking the law if you drive past the road sign that says "Do Not Pass"?
- If you drink Pepsi at work in the Coke factory, will they fire you?
- Why was Evelyn Wood in such a hurry?
- If you're in a vehicle going the speed of light, what happens when you turn on the headlights?
- What happens if you take No-Doze and a sleeping pill at the same time?
- Why don't packages say "Open Somewhere Else"?

- Where does the white go when the snow melts?
- Why aren't there any toothcombs?
- How do you get off a non-stop flight?
- Why don't we say "Holy Salmon"?
- Does anyone actually use those little hangers that socks come on?
- Why is there no Tigers Club?
- If Barbie is so popular, why do you have to buy her friends?
- Why don't kids ever bring goalie gloves to hockey games to catch pucks?
- Do people turn their car lights off during a funeral at night?
- How do you know if honesty is the best policy unless you've tried some of the others?
- What if there were no hypothetical situations?
- How much is a sand dollar worth?
- Why don't trucks make wide left turns?
- Would a plastic surgeon melt if she got too close to a fire?
- How do you write zero in roman numerals?
- Why aren't there any piano donor cards?
- Where is the city of Charter that all those buses are going to?
- Why is there no flower called a zipperdragon?

- Why aren't commercials for closed captioned TV stations closed captioned?

- Do we really need to see the backs of our heads after a haircut?

- Why is it that rain drops and snow falls?

- Wouldn't you think an autobiography would be the life story of a car?

- Why doesn't anyone go "fat dipping"?

- How is it that people always seem to die in alphabetical order?

- Why are they called Amusement Parks when you have to wait in line so long?

- Where would a doorman picket if he went on strike?

- Why is there an ad for the psychic hotline?

- How do you know if your invisible fence was installed?

- Why is there no size extra medium?

- If electricity comes from electrons, does morality come from morons?

- Why do they call it an asteroid when it's outside the hemisphere, but call it a hemorrhoid when it's in your butt?

- Where do you find clean dirt?

- Why is it that to stop Windows 98, you have to click on "Start"?

- Can blind people see their dreams?

Is there anyone with a wet sense of humor?

- How can someone turn-up missing?

- Why do kamikaze pilots wear helmets?

- When people tell you they're giving you an 800 number, why must they start with "800"?

- Why do we camouflage military equipment to fight in the desert?

- Since Americans throw rice at weddings, do Asians throw hamburgers?

- Where does that crust in your eye come from?

- Why do power outages always happen at 12:00?

- How can you put siding on the front of a house?
- Why don't we say "Old Lady Winter" or "Old Lady River"?
- If it's true that we are here to help others, then what exactly are the others here for?
- Why are there no square table discussions?
- Where is Old Zealand?
- When dumb people watch TV, shouldn't they have the brightness level all the way up?
- Why are there mailboxes outside the Post Office?
- What's the difference between a stroll, a mosey, and a saunter?
- Why do they call it life insurance?
- Have you ever asked for a price check at "Everything's A Dollar"?
- Why aren't there any Bed & Brunch lodges for people who like to sleep in?
- Do short golfers yell "two"?
- Why are there interstate highways in Hawaii?
- Which is the other side of the street?
- Is it dyslexic being hell?
- Do bakers feel cheated when they buy 12-packs?
- Why do they call it quicksand when you sink down slowly?

- Where do temporary agencies get their employees?
- Why is it called the funny bone when it hurts after it gets bumped?
- Have you ever lost any sleep over having narcolepsy?
- Why do Realtors put their pictures on signs and business cards?
- If work is so great, how come they have to pay you to do it?
- Is it possible to be totally partial?
- Can you be a closet claustrophobic?
- Why do they lock gas station bathrooms? Are they afraid someone will clean them?
- Why are car mechanics shirts and hands only clean on TV commercials?
- Do bleach blondes pretend to have more fun?
- If a mime gets arrested, do the police tell him he has the right to remain silent?
- What do you do when you see an endangered animal eating endangered plants?
- Do Roman paramedics refer to IV's as "4's"?
- Why do they report power outages on TV?
- Does the French militia use Dijon mustard gas?
- Is it legal to run into a crowded fire and yell "Theater!"?

- Just before someone gets nervous, do they experience cocoons in their stomach?

- If someone has a mid-life crisis while playing hide and seek, does he automatically lose because he can't find himself?

- Is there a group for people who abuse acronyms? If so, what do they call it for short?

- If someone with multiple personalities threatens to kill himself, is it considered a hostage situation?

- Why don't more masked robbers hold up ski lodges?

- How does a person with a lisp pronounce the word?

- Why is there no flower called an evening-glory?

If the # 2 pencil is the most popular, why is it still #2?

- Do clowns wear really big socks?

- If corn oil comes from corn, where does baby oil come from?

- How did a fool and his money get together?
- Do cannibals get hungry one hour after eating a Chinaman?
- How do you know when it's time to tune your bagpipes?
- Do blind Eskimos have seeing eye sled dogs?
- How is it possible to run out of space?
- Do pediatricians play miniature golf on Wednesdays?
- Before they invented drawing boards, what did people go back to?
- Do infants enjoy infancy as much as adults enjoy adultery?
- If a 911 operator has a heart attack, whom does he or she call?
- How long is the long arm of the law?
- If duck season begins in May, when does tourist season open?
- How many weeks are there in a light year?
- If one synchronized swimmer drowns, do the rest have to drown too?
- Why does X stand for a kiss and O for a hug?
- If you're born again, do you have two belly buttons?
- Why don't we ask short people to pick things up off the floor?
- If you try to fail, and succeed, which have you done?
- Why don't our ears get iatated?

- If you've read a book, you can reread it. But wouldn't this also mean that you would have to "member" someone in order to remember them?

- What is a hacky and why is it in a sack?

- If space is a vacuum, who changes the bags?

- Why does the sun lighten our hair, but darken our skin?

- If you save time, when do you get to use it?

- Why is "crazy man" an insult, while to insert a comma and say "Crazy, man!" is a compliment?

- Why is it that writers write but fingers don't fing, grocers don't groce and hammers don't ham?

- If teachers taught, why don't preachers praught?

- Why can we make amends but not one amend?

- If you have a bunch of odds and ends and get rid of all but one of them, what do you call it?

- Why can we comb through the annals of history but not a single annal?

- If a vegetarian eats vegetables, what do humanitarians eat?

- How can the weather be hot as hell one day and cold as hell the next?

- Have you ever seen a horseful carriage or a strapful gown?

- Why is clear considered a color?

- Have you ever met a sung hero or experienced requited love?

- If blind people wear dark glasses, why don't deaf people wear earmuffs?

- Have you ever run into someone who was combobulated, gruntled, ruly or peccable?

- Why is it that a house can burn up as it burns down?

- If everything is part of a whole, what is the whole part of?

- Why is it that you fill in a form by filling it out?

- Since light travels faster than sound, is that why some people appear bright until you hear them speak?

Is a book on failure a success if it doesn't sell?

- If it's zero degrees outside today and it's supposed to be twice as cold tomorrow, how cold is it going to be?

- Why do you press harder on a remote-control when you know the battery is dead?

- If love is blind, why is lingerie so popular?

- Why do banks charge you a "non-sufficient funds fee" on money they already know you don't have?

- Can you lose weight if you dream you are exercising?

- Why do they call it the Department of Interior when they are in charge of everything outdoors?

- How much deeper would the ocean be if sponges didn't grow in it?

- If a tree falls on a mime, does it make a sound?

- Why doesn't Tarzan have a beard?

- How do I set my laser printer to stun?

- If a jogger runs at the speed of sound, can he still hear his Walkman?

- How is it possible to have a civil war?

- If most car accidents occur within five miles of home, why doesn't everyone just move 10 miles away?

- Should crematoriums give discounts for burn victims?

- If a man is standing in the middle of the forest speaking and there is no woman around to hear him, is he still wrong?

- When sign makers go on strike, is anything written on their signs?

- How can someone resign a contract and resign their position?

- If a stealth bomber crashes in a forest, will it make a sound?

- Why are violets blue and not violet?

- If the police arrest a mime, do they tell him he has the right to remain silent?

- Why do you need an appointment to see a psychic?

- If all those psychics know the winning lottery numbers, why are they still working?

- Does the reverse side also have a reverse side?

- If you got into a taxi and he started driving backwards, would the driver end up owing you money?

- How do "Keep off the grass" signs get where they are?

- If time heals all wounds, why don't belly buttons fill in?

- Why is there only one Monopolies commission?

- How do you buy invisible tape?

- When something fades in the sunlight, where do the colors go?

- Where do you park if you work in a hydrant factory?

- If conjoined twins participate in sports, do they count as one or two players?

- Have you ever tried to buy some batteries but they weren't included?

- How do you pull out of a circular driveway?

- How is it that we put man on the moon before we figured out it would be a good idea to put wheels on luggage?

- Do Chinese mothers teach their babies to eat with toothpicks?

Why is the alphabet in that order? Is it because of that song?!

- If you jogged backwards, would you gain weight?

- What would you call a pocket calculator in a nudist camp?

- Why do we lift a thumb to thumb a lift?

- If man evolved from monkeys and apes, why do we still have monkeys and apes?

- Why are boxing rings square?

- Where do forest rangers go to "get away from it all"?

- Instead of talking to your plants, if you yelled at them would they still grow or only be troubled and insecure?

- How important does a person have to be before they are considered assassinated instead of just murdered?

- Why is an actor <u>in</u> a movie but <u>on</u> TV?

- If you wear your contacts while sleeping, can you see your dreams more clearly?

- If Jimmy cracks corn and no one cares, why is there a song about him?

- If the professor on Gilligan's Island can make a radio out of a coconut, why couldn't he fix a hole in a boat?

- What do you call male ballerinas?

- When we say our mind wanders, where does it go?

- If quizzes are quizzical, what are tests?

- Why do mattresses have designs on them when they're always covered with sheets?

- If electricity comes from electrons, does morality come from morons?

- Is Disney World the only people trap operated by a mouse?

- Why do the Alphabet song and Twinkle, Twinkle Little Star have the same tune?

- If 4 out of 5 people suffer from diarrhea, does that mean one actually enjoys it?

- What color hair do they put on the driver's licenses of bald men?

- Ever wonder what the speed of lightning would be if it didn't zigzag?

- Whatever happened to Preparations A through G?

- Can a hearse carrying a corpse drive in the carpool lane?

- When I erase a word with a pencil, where does it go?

- If a singer sings their own song during a karaoke party, is it considered karaoke?

Why doesn't anyone watch their height?

- Can you get cavities in your dentures if you use too much artificial sweetener?

- Why is it called "after dark" when it really is "after light"?

- If you are cross-eyed and have dyslexia, can you read all right?

- Why do we wind a watch to start it and wind up a letter to end it?

- If swimming is so good for you why are whales so big?

- Why don't we ever hear about smart fog?

- What do you call a woman named Sheila in Australia?

- Why does Superman stop bullets with his chest, but ducks when you throw a revolver at him?

- If you can wave a fan, and you can wave a club, why can't you wave a fan club?

- Why are there no corporate innings?

- Should a mute be yelled at for talking with their hands full?

- Why do people keep running over a string a dozen times with their vacuum cleaner, then reach down, pick it up, examine it, then put it down to give the vacuum one more chance?

- Why is it that whenever you attempt to catch something that's falling off the table you always manage to knock something else over?

- How come you never hear father-in-law jokes?

- Why do some men have hair where they don't want it and none where they need it?

- Why do we leave cars worth thousands of dollars in the driveway and put our useless junk in the garage?

Chapter 2 – Animal Antics

- Why do people talk baby talk to young animals?
- Is it smart to help a constipated dog?
- Would you call the lower leg of a cow, a calf?
- Do deer only cross at "Deer Crossing" signs?
- What kind of aid do blind dogs get?
- Why don't you ever see baby pigeons?
- What kind of ball would pigs use if they played football?
- Do radioactive cats have 18 half-lives?
- Do jellyfish get gas from eating jellybeans?
- What if white mice caused cancer?
- How can a rabbit's foot be lucky? They have four of them and they're hunted, hit by cars, and put in soup?
- Is it appropriate to say "hop in" to a kangaroo hitchhiking?
- Have you ever seen a toad on a toadstool?
- Is the illness a giraffe dreads most a sore throat?
- Do horses ever feel like making bets on human track events?
- Have you ever seen deer and antelope playing?
- Do man-eating sharks eat women to?

- Have you ever heard of a fraidy dog?

- Why isn't there a bird a little bigger than a swallow called a gulp?

- There's a hummingbird, but is there a bird that actually knows the words?

- Why isn't there a peanut butter fish?

- After eating, do amphibians have to wait one hour before getting out of the water?

- Why are there no goatdogs?

Would a neurotic owl say

- Does skim milk come from anorexic cows?

- Should you give sick chickens, people soup?

- Do turtles use people wax to shine their shells?

- If humans get a charley horse, what do horses get?

- What do penguins wear for play clothes?

- Do squirrel monkeys eat nuts?

- Why does Donald Duck wear a towel after showering when he doesn't normally wear pants?

- Do turtle doves fly slower than other birds?

- Has anyone ever seen a partridge in a pear tree?

- Why isn't there a Dr. Shark?

- Have you ever seen a flock of clay pigeons?

- Why do flamingos stand on only one leg?

- Have you ever seen a barrel of monkeys?

- Does virgin wool come from ugly sheep?

- Why can't you buy four quarter horses for a dollar?

- Do turtles wear people-neck sweaters?

- Have you ever seen a pigeon that is people-toed?

- What would happen if a rattlesnake bit its tongue?

- Do black cows give chocolate milk?

- Does distressed leather come from very tense cows?

- Why aren't there any bird showers?

- Does the person who inventories sheep often fall asleep on the job?

- Why aren't there toupees made of feathers for bald eagles?

- Do indecisive squids discharge erasable ink?

- What do little birdies see when they get knocked unconscious?

- If alligators wore shirts, would they have people on them?

- Why don't you ever see hedgehogs in bushes?

- When ducks take baths, do they have rubber people floating around?

- If ducks had payments to make, would they be called lips?

- Why is Mickey Mouse bigger than his dog Pluto?

- If a goose got a chill, would it get people bumps?

- When sheep can't sleep do they count people?

- If ducks went hunting, what would a human call sound like?

- When ducks are dodging bullets, do they shout "human" at each other?

- What do you feed a Christmas seal?

- Do crocodiles ever shed human tears?

- Why do pigs have curly tails?

- What does an elephant have to remember?

- If humans have nightmares, what do horses have?

- What part of a horse is in horseradish?

- Do chickens ever get people pox?

- Should animal shampoo be tested on humans?

- Do bears have people-skin rugs in front of their fireplaces?

- Why don't birds grow from bird seed?

- When cows laugh does milk come out of their noses?

- Has anyone ever seen a weasel go "pop"?

Could dogs enter their masters in a "people show"?

- Do those poker playing dogs own paintings of humans playing "fetch"?

- Could you make a rug out of a Persian cat?

- Why isn't there a bird called a queenfisher?

- Could you make a blanket out of an afghan dog?

- Why isn't there a devil fish?
- Do horses play H-U-M-A-N?
- Why don't bullfrogs have horns?
- What time exactly do cows come home?
- Why is there no Alaskan queen crab?
- Why do dogs stick their heads out of moving car windows, and then get annoyed when you blow in their faces?
- Do rabbits ever make people shadows?
- Why don't people take dog naps?
- Could electric eels ever convert to gas?
- Why doesn't the Boxer dog come in different weight classes?
- Why aren't there any bulldog fights?
- Why is it called horsepower when it has nothing to do with horses?
- Do pigs keep their money in people banks?
- If you tied buttered toast to the back of a cat and dropped him, what would happen?
- Would you call a lousy Doctor that is a duck, a quack?
- How would pigeons react to a statue of a cat in the park?
- Do hunting dogs carry guns?

- What do mock turtles eat?
- Why is there no seahorse racing?
- What would you call a Siamese cat with two heads?
- Can you only catch a rainbow trout when it's sunny and raining?
- Why do they call it 'getting your dog fixed' when afterwards it doesn't work anymore?
- Has a monkey ever even used a wrench?
- Why are there no winter chickens?
- Do horses like to play H-U-M-A-N?
- Why don't sheep shrink when it rains?
- Why do cats all of a sudden have to be in another room?
- After eating, do amphibians have to wait one hour before getting out of the water?
- Do chickens think rubber humans are funny?
- Has an elephant ever been diagnosed with humantitis?
- If a turtle doesn't have a shell, is he homeless or naked
- Do fish get cramps after eating?
- Is boneless chicken considered to be an invertebrate?
- If Wile E. Coyote had enough money to buy all that Acme stuff, why didn't he just buy food?
- Why is a guinea pig neither from Guinea nor is it a pig?

- What do dust bunnies eat?

- Why do worms come out after it rains?

- How come birds can fly but flies can't bird?

- Does anyone really know why the chicken crossed the road?

- Why does Goofy stand erect while Pluto remains on all fours? They're both dogs!

Chapter 3 – Food For Fun

- Why do hot dogs come in packages of ten and buns in eights?
- Are beans shaped like kidneys or is the kidney shaped like a bean?
- Why does it take "Minute Rice" five minutes to cook?
- When cheese gets its picture taken, what does it say?
- Why is it called "chili" when it's hot and spicy?
- What is "soft liquor"?
- Why is there no fresh water taffy?
- How much milk is there in the Milky Way?
- Why are there no hot cats?
- If an orange is orange, why isn't a lime called a green and a lemon called a yellow?
- Why do we say "tuna" fish, but not "trout" fish?
- How come eggplant isn't white?
- Why is a pear only one?
- Can Gouda cheese be bad?
- Should beer nuts be served to minors?
- Why do they sell a pound cake that only weighs 12 ounces?

- Why does mineral water that 'has trickled through the mountains for centuries' have a 'use by' date?

- How can you have a home cooked meal at a restaurant?

- Should short people use condensed milk?

- Why isn't there lettuce in potato or fruit salad?

What was the best thing before sliced bread?

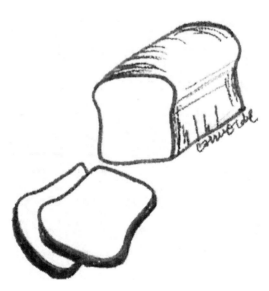

- Should basketball players eat anything with shortening?

- Why doesn't Swiss steak have holes in it?

- Why don't restaurants serve chicken pot pie a la mode?

- Why aren't there any army beans?

- Can wax beans be used as candles?

- Why is grapefruit yellow?

- Why can't you blow bubbles with gumdrops?

- How do you get evaporated milk into a can?
- How long does it take to cook minute steak?
- Why aren't there any peanut butter filled doughnuts?
- Is it okay to drink juice with coffee cake?
- Why are fruitcakes only served around Christmas time?
- Why isn't there any margarine milk?
- Do Danish people have American rolls for breakfast?
- Would people on a diet eat petit twos?
- How come we put vanilla in chocolate cake?
- Why is there no chicken a la queen?
- Why are there no hayberries?
- Why isn't there a low calorie salad dressing called "100 Island"?
- Do wealthy people eat Charles roast?
- Can wheat germ make you sick?
- Why do they call it "tuna fish?" They don't call chicken "chicken bird".
- Could it be baking soda that makes refrigerators smell bad?
- Why aren't there any peanut butter beans?
- There's a Mars bar, why isn't there a Venus or Saturn bar?
- Why isn't there drinking and dancing at a salad bar?

- Why is there no cheese in cheesecake?
- Would you go back in time if you put instant coffee in the microwave?
- Is it catsup or ketchup?
- Why is cheese so secret that we must shred it?
- If you spilled a dry martini, would anything get wet?
- Could you polish your car with wax beans?
- Why is most lunchmeat bigger than the bread?
- If you buried an eggplant, would a chicken grow?
- Could you use sponge cake to wipe up a spill?
- Would eating Froot Loops or Cheez Whiz affect your spelling ability?
- Why do we refry beans and bake potatoes twice?
- What do forest preserves taste like?
- Can you eat summer sausage in the spring?
- Wouldn't you think they made chocolate at the US Mint?
- Why is there no knee macaroni?
- Wouldn't it make sense to have butt-flavored cat food?
- What do the manufacturers of Half and Half do with the other 1/2 and 1/2?
- Why does it seem like diet foods make people fat?

- Should fruitcakes be served at Psychiatric Hospitals?
- Is it okay to put cough syrup on pancakes?
- Why are they called raisins if they are only dried grapes?
- Is it okay to eat a sundae on a Tuesday?

Can egg foo young ever get old?

- If white wine goes with fish, do white grapes go with sushi?
- What do chefs do with frog arms?
- How do you know when yogurt goes bad?
- Are pink lemons used in pink lemonade?
- Why isn't there any queen salmon?
- Why is there an expiration date on sour cream?
- What kind of fruit is in Juicy Fruit gum?

- Why is lemon juice made with artificial flavor, while dishwashing liquid is made with real lemons?

- Why does seafood cost more the closer you are to the water?

- Should you eat turtle soup slower?

- Why is food that sticks to your teeth bad, and food that sticks to your ribs good?

- Why is Canada Dry wet?

- Was Julius Caesar the first person to eat a salad?

- Isn't cheese food redundant?

- Why doesn't grilled cheese have black lines on it?

- Have you ever wanted to order some eggs and chicken at a restaurant and see which one comes first?

- Why are carrots not called oranges, as they are more orange than oranges?

- Do illiterate people get the full effect of alphabet soup?

- Why are there no rice pies?

- Should fast food restaurants be allowed to serve escargot?

- If you ate pasta and antipasta, would you still be hungry?

- Why is there neither egg in eggplant, nor ham in hamburger nor neither pine nor apple in pineapple?

- Why are they called English muffins when they weren't invented in England?

- Why are they called French Fries whey they weren't invented in France?

- Why are they called sweetbreads when they are not sweet and are actually meat?

- Since bread is square, why is some sandwich meat round?

- Why does round pizza come in a square box?

- Why is there no corn in corned beef?

- What is a refried bean? Why do they have to fry it twice?

- Why aren't French fries considered a vegetable, they are just deep fried potatoes?

- When dog food is "new and improved" who tastes it?

- Why do croutons come in airtight packages? Aren't they just stale bread to begin with?

Chapter 4 – Cliché Quandaries

- Why don't people say "We live in a cat eat cat world"?

- How can someone "draw a blank"?

- What would happen if it did rain cats and dogs?

- If old people are considered "over the hill", why don't we call dead people "under the hill"?

- Why don't people ask "Dog got your tongue"?

- Can someone have their head in the clouds and be down-to-earth at the same time?

- What happens if you get scared half to death twice?

- How do we really know how old dirt is?

- Why doesn't anyone ever get as sick as a cat?

- If quitters never win, and winners never quit, who is the genius that came up with, "Quit while you're ahead"?

- Why don't people say "That's the dog's bark"?

- If something is "needless to say", why is it always said?

- Aren't a fat chance and slim chance the same thing?

- Why doesn't anyone ever "hit the straw"?

- Why doesn't anyone shed alligator tears?

- Do fishermen often bait and switch?

Are buttons really that cute?

- Do really ambitious people go the whole ten yards?

- Wouldn't a baby choke if it was born with silver spoon in its mouth?

- Has anyone actually killed two birds with one stone?

- Why isn't there a "rule of pinky"?

- Have you ever been on a wild goose chase?

- Why isn't anyone ever said to be "all pinkys"?

- How can the weather be "hot as hell" one day and "cold as hell" another?

- Why don't we ask happy people "Why the short face?"

- Do cats and dogs fight like people?

- Who bars the door when Katie isn't around?

- Can blind people see things "eye to eye"?
- Would not so happy people just be on "cloud 3"?
- How do we know logs sleep soundly?
- Do hotcakes really sell that well?
- Has anyone ever "gotten your sheep"?
- Does your masseuse often rub you the wrong way?
- Has anyone ever tried the "hair of the cat" for a hangover remedy?
- Why don't we say, "It's a cat's life"?
- If an apple a day keeps a Dr. away, would a watermelon a day keep a lawyer away?
- Has anyone ever barked up the correct tree?
- Why doesn't anyone ever "beat around the shrub"?
- Is sliced bread really that great?
- How can someone be beside themselves?
- Do pigs that work bring home the flesh?
- How did the bull get into the china shop?
- Who's canning all these worms that people are opening up?
- Why don't we say "has the dog got your tongue"?
- Are there any hearing aids for posts?

- Where do skunks get their alcohol?

- Is "tired old cliché" one?

- Why is nothing as easy as cake?

- Should you ever speak the words "you can say that again" to someone who stutters?

If all the world's a stage, where is the <u>audience</u> sitting?

- When will every cat have his day?

- Are clams really that happy?

- Why doesn't anyone mind their "A's and B's"?
- Do prosperous hogs live high off the human?
- Why do you have to wait until night to call it a day?
- Do smart horses have human sense?
- Doesn't it take two to dance any dance?
- Where do the Joneses live and why should we keep up with them?
- Shouldn't we let sleeping cats lie too?
- If your left hand doesn't know what your right one is doing, shouldn't you be getting more sleep?
- Has anyone ever gotten a right-handed compliment?
- What happens when you swallow your pride?
- Has the dog ever been let out of the bag?
- Why isn't life ever a bowl of oranges?
- Has anyone actually shot any fish in a barrel?
- Where is this little bird, and why does he keep gossiping?
- How many ways are there to skin a cat?
- Is a pin really that neat?
- How did the needle get in the haystack?
- Why don't we say "That's not my cup of coffee"?

- A stitch in time saves nine what?
- Why don't people say "This is a cat day afternoon"?
- Have you ever heard chairs playing music?
- Would you get more out of a person if you gave them a quarter for their thoughts?
- Has anyone ever seen a rat race?
- Do massage therapists ever rub people the wrong way?
- If a picture is worth a thousand words, what is a picture of a thousand words worth?
- Do nerds always eat square meals?
- What was the best thing before sliced bread?
- Why do you have to put your two cents in, but it's only a penny for your thoughts? Where does the other penny go?
- Can you start up a fitness center with just sweat equity?
- When car mechanics get angry, do they blow a gasket?
- Why is it that people say they "slept like a baby" when babies wake up about every two hours?
- Doesn't "expecting the unexpected" make the unexpected expected?
- Why aren't there any cash horses?
- Has anyone ever "kicked the pail"?
- Are cats' woman's best friend?

Chapter 5 – Insect Insights

- Why is there an insect called an ant but not an uncle?
- What do you call a male ladybug?
- Are female moths called myths?
- What if a praying mantis turned atheist?
- Why is there no insect called a thunder bug?
- How do those dead bugs get into those enclosed light fixtures?
- What do potato bugs eat?
- Why is there no insect called mommy long legs?
- Why is there no margarine fly?
- Was there a dragonfly in medieval times?
- What does a fruit fly eat?
- Why is there no insect called a walking twig?
- Do wolf spiders howl?
- Why didn't Noah swat those two mosquitoes?
- Why is there no insect called a tock?
- Are there any fire-breathing dragonflies?
- Why is there no apartment fly?
- Has anyone actually bought a flea at the market?

- Have you ever been bitten by a bed bug?
- Why are there no navy ants?
- Have you ever seen a junebug in April or a mayfly in July?
- Have you ever gotten moths in your stomach?
- Do roach motels have free cable movies?
- What kind of livestock is there on an ant farm?
- Do fleas wear dog collars?
- Were inch worms made to convert to the metric system?
- What do insects say when they get mad at each other, "bug off"?
- Why do worms come out after it rains?
- If you ate a pill bug, would your headache go away?
- Why aren't fat walking sticks called walking branches?
- Is there such thing as dried fruit flies?
- Katydid what?
- What happens when none of your bees wax?
- Are damselflies ever in distress?
- Why aren't lazy grasshoppers called grasswalkers?
- If a fly didn't have wings, would it be called a walk?
- Why are there no "Deer Tick Crossing" signs?

- Would you ever name your pet goliath beetle David?

- How do those dead bugs get into those enclosed light fixtures?

Chapter 6 - PUNS TO PONDER

- Why isn't there a sky diving board?

- If the Supremes were playing racquetball, would you say they're on the Supreme Court?

- Are gavels made from judicial branches?

- If babies went to school, would they take crib notes?

- Can you write a letter on a stationary bike?

- I have a bad case of kleptomania, what should I take for it?

- Have ex-mathematicians become dysfunctional?

- Is there a Ceiling Fan Club?

- Do plumbers get tired of being at everyone's disposal?

- If your nose went on strike, would you help picket?

- When a pony gets a sore throat and can't speak, should you say it's a little horse?

- If a young dog wanted to go camping would it use a pup tent?

- Why don't all bay windows overlook water?

- Could lazy people use forklifts to eat?

- Does the Postmaster General need a stamp of approval?

- If a chicken was playing baseball and hit a ball out of play, would you call it a fowl ball?

- What would you call it if a pig used karate on someone, a pork chop?

- If fish went to war, would they use fish tanks?

- Do dog kennels have "No Barking Zones"?

- Are frogs ever afraid of croaking?

Do archeologists listen to rock music?

- If a person thinks marathons are superior to sprints, is that racism?

- What do you call a piece of rabbit meat, a hare cut?

- Do witches run spell checkers?
- Would you go to Alaska just for the halibut?
- Are carpenters required to eat pound cake?
- If a ducks wing fell off, would duct tape fix it?
- Do phone operators use Dial?
- Who would play shortstop on a midget baseball team?
- If you left a saw lying around, would it collect saw dust?
- Have ex-locomotive engineers been derailed?
- Would you call a sculpture of a woman's chest, a bust?
- Does a sleeping bag ever wake up?
- If you chipped a tooth, would toothpaste fix it?
- Would tomato paste work to fix broken tomatoes?
- Is the nose the scenter of the face?
- What do you call it when a cat throws garbage everywhere, kitty litter?
- Would it be called a "royal flush" after a king or queen used the bathroom?
- What do you call Robin Hood's mother, Mother Hood?
- Can you fish with a bookworm?
- Did Dr. Freud's wife wear Freudian slips?

- If a librarian retrains as a barber, does that person become a barbarian?
- Can only people who are in the Armed Forces wear tank tops?
- Do athletes ever grow when they plant their feet?
- When a wife leaves her farmer husband, does she leave him a John Deere letter?
- Do carpenters usually have hammer toes?
- If a seagull flew over the bay, would it be called a bagel?
- Do gymnasts usually live in houses with vaulted ceilings?
- If big elephants have big trunks, do small elephants have suitcases?
- Did Casper ever have a ghoulfriend?
- If a dog has ticks, is it considered a watch dog?
- Do most carpenters drink screwdrivers?
- Is an ascot a tie or a little donkey's bed?
- What do you call a bull that sleeps a lot, a bulldozer?
- Do people in the Marines tend to eat more submarine sandwiches?
- If you fell through a screen door, would you strain yourself?
- Do most baseball pitchers eat Mounds bars?
- Why is it that night falls but day breaks?

- If there were two pirates sitting across from one another would they be seeing "Aye to Aye"?

- Do boxers drink a lot of punch?

- If you accidentally washed a dollar bill, would that be money laundering?

- What would you call a religious person who like snack foods, a chip Monk?

- Do spider monkeys spin webs?

- If a comedian took off all his clothes, would that be a comic strip?

- Have you ever asked a music store clerk for a compact disc, and then they go and kick you in the back?

- Is loose leaf paper more available in the fall?

- What if your masseuse rubs you the wrong way?

- How often do carpenters use construction paper on their projects?

- Do audio store experts always give sound advice?

- If one chicken sent money to another, would that be a chicken wire?

- Can an ambidextrous person make an off hand remark?

- If fruit could be in the Armed Forces, would there be an Apple Corp?

- Would you say a small boat with no brains is a little dinghy?

- Do hardware stores have drill teams?
- Have ex-civil lawyers become distorted?
- How long do snow tires last before they melt?
- Do cosmetologists ever have to take make-up tests?
- If Dracula turned into a dog, would he be called a bloodhound?
- Do you feed a boogie fever?
- Are you telling the truth if you lie in bed?
- If Cap'n Crunch was fatally shot, would that be a cereal killing?
- Are part-time band leaders called semi-conductors?
- If a bunch of rabbits were in a row and each took a step backwards, would that be a receding hare line?
- Is a small pig called a hamlet?
- How many days can ice go without shaving?
- If two spiders got married, would they be considered newlywebs?
- Do skunks have common scents?
- If a deaf person has to go to court, is it still called a hearing?
- Do you think Rich Little wants to make a good first impression?
- When sugar company executives travel, do they have to stay in suites?

- Do most people who get into the monogram business have initial success?

- If you cross a goat and an owl, will you get a hootenanny?

- Do publishers choose books that are bound to do well?

- If a shoe store is owned by one person, would that be considered a Sole Proprietorship?

- Did Noah keep his bees in arkhives?

- If Sir Lancelot had a bad dream about a horse, would that be considered a knight-mare?

Do cruise ships have car control?

- Shouldn't married couples stay away from waterbeds so they don't drift apart?

- Why get even when you can get odd?

- If a person swallowed a contact lens, would that give them better insight?

- Would a sheep go to the Bah-Bah shop to get sheared?

- Do personal injury lawyers normally name their daughters "Sue"?

- If you cross a dove with a high chair, will you get a stool pigeon?

- What do topless bars do when it rains?

- Do very emotional people drive "Saabs"?

- Should people who wear glasses be allowed to play contact sports?

- Is Mt. Fuji where all the film comes from?

- Have you ever stared at a can of orange juice because it says "concentrate" on it?

- If you stepped on a watch and broke it, would that be just killing time?

- Do electricians ever get grounded?

- Is it okay to listen to an AM radio station after noon?

- Wouldn't it be easier to just buy a zipper than to go fly fishing?

- Have ex-bankers become disinterested?

- Do shy turtles ever come out of their shell?

- If you took a refresher class at an Aviation School, should it be called a crash course?

- Do most cowboys like ranch dressing on their salads?

- Is it okay to play soccer in tennis shoes?

- Can you buy an entire chess set at a pawnshop?
- Do people who work at the IRS live in tax shelters?
- There's a tongue depressor, but is there anything to cheer a tongue up?
- Are crop tops just T-shirts with corn on them?
- If flowers don't talk back to you, are they mums?
- Do hunters usually shop at Target?
- Can only certain football players use Right Guard?
- Do members of the Audubon Society have extra tweeters in their speakers?
- If two vampires were mad at each other, would that be considered bad blood?
- Do Anglers often have bated breath?
- Does fly paper make better airplanes and kites?
- Why do we sing hymns but not hers at church?
- Shouldn't penny loafers be less expensive than other shoes?
- Why are builders afraid of a 13th floor, but publishers not afraid of a chapter 11?
- Should mentally unstable people be allowed to eat nuts?
- If a pig is sold to a pawn shop, is it a ham-hock?
- Do graffiti artists often see the handwriting on the wall?

- If you cross a ten foot pole with a cat, will you get a ten foot pole cat?
- Do garage door companies have any overhead?
- Could an animal that loses its tail get help from a retail store?
- Don't veterinarians give pet-icures?
- Can you get in shape by exercising your rights?
- If you saw a heat wave, would you wave back?
- Was Bozo a class clown?
- Is it considered an empty nest when a mother bird's young all leave?
- Can you recognize a dogwood tree by its bark?
- Does California have a lot of "dude" ranches?
- Do carpenters go to saw horse races?
- Is it possible to teach a pet peeve tricks?
- Have ex-punsters been expunged?
- Do horse racers wear Jockey underwear?
- Are Dentists always down in the mouth?
- Why would anyone want to watch Greyhound buses race?
- How many trees does it take to make a fir coat?
- Do vampires eat steak?

- When day breaks who fixes it?

- Do hungry crows have ravenous appetites?

- If a parsley farmer is sued, can they garnish his wages?

- If you called a Chinese restaurant by mistake, would that be a Wong number?

- Should boats with kitchens have sinks?

- Do electricians who get into trouble end up in circuit court?

- Is an oxymoron a really dumb bovine?

- Do cured hams ever get sick?

- How does a person clean up noise pollution?

- Do Japanese people wok their dogs?

- Has anyone ever brought in a chair when asked for a stool sample?

- Is it true that cannibals don't eat clowns because they taste funny?

- Have you ever seen an alley cat when bowling?

- Would cows that have been in earthquakes give milkshakes?

- Are codfish balls informal or black tie?

- Should depressed people wear down coats?

- Do gardeners get plantars warts very often?

- Why don't outlet stores sell electrical fixtures?

- Is it true that atheism is a non-prophet organization?

- If money doesn't grow on trees then why do banks have branches?

- Does killing time damage eternity?

- If lawyers are disbarred and clergymen defrocked, doesn't it follow that electricians can be delighted, musicians denoted, cowboys deranged, models deposed, tree surgeons debarked and dry cleaners depressed?

- Is it good if a vacuum really sucks?

- Does Tom Thumb have a younger brother named Pinky?

- Is a pessimist's blood type always b-negative?

If two candles are dating, should you say that they're going out together?

- Would you call a lizard with a lot of money a chameleonairre?

- Is a hangover considered the wrath of grapes?

- Do tennis pro shop owners ever get arrested for racketeering?

- Is it true that sleeping on corduroy pillows makes headlines?

- What kind of stuffing do taxidermists have for Thanksgiving?

- Is a book on voyeurism a peeping tome?

- When night falls, who picks it up?

- Is it true that marriage is the mourning after the knot before?

- Did you hear that sea captains don't like crew cuts?

- Does the name Pavlov ring a bell?

- Is it true that a successful diet is the triumph of mind over platter?

- Why do we wait until a pig is dead to cure it?

- If time flies like an arrow, do fruit flies like bananas?

- How many full buckets are allowed when ice fishing?

- Is it true that a gossip is someone with a great sense of rumor?

- Did you know that without geometry, life would be pointless?

- If you dream in color, would that be considered a pigment of your imagination?

- Do church leaders who workout like to do preacher curls?
- Is it true that reading while sunbathing can make you well-red?
- Did you know that when two egotists meet, it's an I for an I?
- Does a backwards poet write inverse?
- Is it true a bicycle can't stand on its own because it's two-tired?
- How can health clubs afford to have "free" weights?
- If in a democracy your vote counts, in feudalism does your count vote?
- Could it be said that a chicken crossing the road is poultry in motion?
- Is it true that if you don't pay your exorcist, you get repossessed?
- When a woman gets married, is it true she gets a new name and a dress?
- Can fat people go skinny dipping?
- When a clock is hungry, does it go back four seconds?
- Should tall people be allowed to play miniature golf?
- Did you hear about the man who fell into an upholstery machine but fully recovered?
- Is it true that a Local Area Network in Australia is called the LAN down under?

- Did you know that a boiled egg in the morning is hard to beat?

- Is it true that once you've seen one shopping center, you've seen a mall?

- Did you hear about the short fortuneteller who escaped from prison and became a small medium at large?

- Is it true that bakers trade bread recipes on a knead-to-know basis?

- Are Santa's helpers called subordinate clauses?

- Is it true that marathon runners with bad footwear suffer the agony of defeat?

- Did you hear that those who jump off a Paris bridge are in Seine?

- Is acupuncture considered a jab well done?

- Does condensed milk come from smaller cows?

- Do they have coffee breaks at the Lipton Tea Company?

- Has anyone ever lost a shadow boxing match?

- Is it legal to drink and "drive" on a golf course?

- What kind of sound does a writing instrument make?

- How can feet smell, they don't have noses?

- Should the "Knights of the Round Table" be allowed to square dance?

- Why do stores advertise sales that are already over like, "Big Sale-Last Week"?

- What do you call a starving artist after they have had a Thanksgiving meal?

- Is the furniture smaller in a juvenile court?

- Does the Little Mermaid wear an algebra?

- How can a door be a jar?

- What happens if you don't perspire while wearing a sweatshirt?

- If you planted a light bulb would a lamp grow?

- Would a blind tourist use a sightseeing eye dog?

- Why don't ranch style homeowners have any livestock?

- When Chinese people get mad at each other, do they "choo" each other out?

- Do spiders spend a lot of time on websites?

- If a deaf person has to go to court, is it still called a hearing?

- If Fed Ex and UPS were to merge, would they call it Fed UP?

- Do young horses wear ponyshoes?

Chapter 7 - Word Wisdom

- Why is it called a fast when it goes by so slowly?
- Isn't a near miss a near hit?
- Why does "slow down" and "slow up" mean the same thing?
- Is progress the opposite of Congress?
- Why are quite a lot and quite a few the same?
- Shouldn't buildings be called builts because they're finished?
- Why is it called a restroom when there's little or no resting being done?
- How come they don't call moustaches mouthbrows?
- Why is the plural of goose-geese and not the plural of moose-meese?
- Why isn't "palindrome" spelled the same way backwards?
- Why are there 5 syllables in the word "monosyllabic"?
- How can overlook and oversee be opposites?
- Why are they called apartments when they're so close together?
- If a pronoun is a word used in place of a noun, is a proverb a word used in place of a verb>
- Why do we use the initials TV for television, but not TP for telephone?
- Why is it called a TV set when you only get one?

- Why does "cleave" mean both split apart and stick together?
- What is "ado" and why shouldn't there be any more of it?
- Why are they called stairs inside but steps outside?
- Isn't there a better name for a kind of footwear than slippers?

What's another word for "synonym"?

- Why don't they call taxi drivers taxidermists?
- Shouldn't a wake maybe be called a sleep?
- Why is the word dictionary in the dictionary?
- How come quite a lot and quite a few mean the same thing?
- Why are they called speed bumps when they're supposed to slow you down?
- Why is it called a bust when it stops right before the part it is named after?
- Why does flammable and inflammable mean the same thing?
- What does A.C.R.O.N.Y.M. stand for?

- Why is Joey short for Joe when Joey has more letters?

- How come we call underwear "briefs" when they're worn all day?

- Shouldn't airport hallways be called something different than terminals?

- Why do "cool" and "hot" mean the same thing?

- How come the plural of tooth is teeth and not the plural of booth - beeth?

- Why does "slow up" and "slow down" mean the same thing?

- If a word is misspelled in the dictionary, how would we ever know?

- Why is abbreviated such a long word?

- How come a wise man and wise guy are opposites?

- Why is it so hard to remember how to spell MNEMONIC?

- How come no word in the English language rhymes with month, orange, silver or purple?

- Why is it that when you transport something by car it's called a shipment, but when you transport something by ship it's called cargo?

- Why isn't the word "gullible" in the dictionary?

- What's another word for Thesaurus?

- Why is chili usually hot, Chile is hot, but the word chilly means cold?

- If two mouses are mice and two louses are lice, why aren't two houses hice?

- Why is big a smaller word and small a bigger word?

- In Chinese, why are the words for crisis and opportunity the same?

- Why isn't eleven called onety-one?

- Is it a coincidence that the only 15 letter word that can be spelled without repeating a letter is uncopyrightable?

- Why doesn't "onomatopoeia" sound like what it is?

- Where do swear words come from?

- Why can't you make another word using all the letters in "anagram"?

- If people from Poland are called Poles, why aren't people from Holland called Holes?

- Why is a person who plays the piano called a pianist but a person who drives a racecar is not called a racist?

- How come overlook and oversee mean opposite things?

- If Webster wrote the first dictionary, where did he find all the words?

- Why is "phonics" not spelled the way it sounds?

- Why is it called lipstick if you can still move your lips after applying it?

- Why are they called waiters and waitresses when the customer does all the waiting?

- Why is an army called an infantry if you have to be over 18 to get in?

- Why is it called a rainbow, it's not a bow on top of rain. Why not rain prism?

- Why is non-fiction something true and fiction something not true?

- Why does mono-syllabic have so many syllables?

- Why is the man who invests all your money called a broker?

Chapter 8 – Human Habits

- Why do women go to the bathroom in groups and then complain about how crowded it was?

- Do people who wear sweaters around their necks also wear socks tied around their ankles?

- Why do people who know the least know it the loudest?

- Do people really need to be told how to wash their hair on the back of a shampoo bottle?

- Why do people have to talk to birds in pet stores?

- Do you know of anyone who has been thrown out of an express lane at a grocery store for having more than ten items?

- Why do we say something is out of whack? What is a whack?

- Why do people order double cheeseburgers, large fries and a DIET coke?

- Why do we say something's out of order when it's broken but we never say in of order when it works?

- Wouldn't you just once like to hear a game show contestant say, "I have a jerk for a husband and two ugly children"?

- Why do gynecologists leave the room when you get undressed?

- Why is it that when you're driving and looking for an address, you turn down the radio?

- Why do people try to fool themselves by setting their clocks ahead?

- Why do Dentists ask you questions when they have their fingers in your mouth?

- How come parents yell at their children, and then ask, "Do you hear me"?

- Why do ballet dancers always dance on their toes? Wouldn't it be easier to just hire taller dancers?

- Why do young twins have to be dressed the same?

- Why do people use the word "irregardless"?

- Why do people hang their arms outside their vehicles when driving?

- Why does someone believe you when you say there are four billion stars but check when you say the paint is wet?

- Why do people play at recitals, but recite at plays?

- How come people constantly return to the refrigerator with hopes that something new to eat will have materialized?

- Why do we "moo" at cows whenever we see them?

- Why do people pay to go up tall buildings and then put money in binoculars to look at things on the ground?

- How come we choose from just two people for President and fifty for Miss America?

- Why do scientists call it "re"search when looking for something new?

- In winter why do we try to keep the house as warm as it was in summer when we complained about the heat?

If something is "needless to say," why is it always said?

- Do passengers on planes need to be shown how to use a seat belt?

- Why don't people at car dealerships show their customers how to use a seat belt?

- Why does yawning seem to be contagious?

- Shouldn't people say "don't get stupid" instead of "don't get smart" with me?

- Why do adults have such a hard time with childproof bottles?

- How can hosts and hostesses look straight at two people and ask "How many are you"?

- Why do we talk louder and slower to people who don't understand English?

- Does repeatedly pushing buttons on an elevator make them go faster?

- Why do people pay to go up tall buildings and then put money in binoculars to look at things on the ground?

- Is the best thing about egotists the fact that they don't talk about other people?

- Why do chefs wear such tall hats?

- Why do we light matches to get rid of smells?

- How come baseball managers wear team uniforms?

- Why do we sing "Take me out to the ball game" when we are already there?

- Why do children spell farm E-I-E-I-O?

- How come we celebrate George Washington and Abraham Lincoln's birthday with a mattress sale?

- Why do people remember where they were when someone famous was killed? (Do they have to prove an alibi?)

- Why can't women put on mascara with their mouth closed?

- Why do pharmacies make the sick walk all the way to the back of the store to get prescriptions while healthy people can buy cigarettes at the front counter?

- Why do people tell you when they are speechless?

- How come people go to the unemployment office to find a job?

- Why is it that whenever you attempt to catch something that's falling off the table you always manage to knock something else over?

- Why do parents tell their children not to stick sharp objects in their mouths, and then make them go to the Dentist who does just that?

- Why do we celebrate Labor Day by not working?

- How come scolding parents only count to three?

- Why do we wash bath towels? Aren't we clean when we use them?

- Isn't it unnerving that doctors call what they do "practice"?

- Why do people put arrows at the bottom of their letters?

- Have you noticed that we talk about certain things only when they are absent?

- Why do kids lift up their clothing when they get embarrassed?

- Why do people turn their blinkers on after they are already in the turn only lane?

- Why do athletes only say "Hi" to their mothers when on TV?

- Why do people post signs that say "Lots For Sale", but then don't tell us what's for sale?

Chapter 9 – Inanimate Issues

- Do wall light fixtures really need to say "On" and "Off"?

- Why are all blackboards called that when some of them are green?

- What's the difference between a hat and a cap?

- Why do we need training bras? What can we teach them?

- Where does one sock go when it escapes from the dryer?

- Why are waiting room magazines so old?

- How much more can laundry detergents be new and improved?

- Why do mattresses have springs if they aren't made for jumping on?

- Have you ever used the mince, puree, or frappe' settings on your blender?

- Why doesn't glue stick to the inside of the bottle?

- Can you use Travelers Checks in your hometown?

- Before television, were there frozen radio dinners?

- Why is the third hand on a watch called the second hand?

- Are pads of paper that don't say "legal pad" on them illegal?

- Why isn't there a Mrs. Coffee appliance?

- Does that screwdriver belong to Phillip?

- What's the sound a name makes before it is dropped?
- Why are antiques so old?
- On a driveway sealer container, is it necessary to include the words "use with adequate ventilation"?
- What would happen if you set a cup of tea on a coffee table?
- Why are there locks on screen doors?
- Do files get embarrassed when they get unzipped?
- Why does a dish towel get wet when it dries?
- What does a semi-truck have to do to become a full truck?
- Why aren't planes and black boxes made of the same material?
- How does a Kleenex tissue know when to lay flat or pop up?
- What is the diameter of a square?
- Why do tug boats push their barges?
- How does a thermos know when to keep a liquid hot or cold?
- Why would anyone want to buy unfinished furniture? What good is a chair with only three legs?
- Why do toasters always have a setting that burns the bread which no human being would eat?
- Are burned out light bulbs used in photographers' darkrooms?
- Why do steam irons have a permanent press setting?

- Why do they give you a tape to watch on your new VCR that tells you how to use it?

- What is the difference between a coat, a jacket, and a parka?

- If you had to ship styrofoam, what would you pack it in?

- Why do we put suits in a garment bag and garments in a suitcase?

Why is there no soap at wedding & baby showers?

- Could it be that boulders are statues of big rocks?

- Why do they make cars go so fast it's illegal?

- How can you have uneven parallel bars?

- Why are they called stands when they are made for sitting?

- What do batteries run on?

- Why is it that whatever color of bubble bath you use the bubbles are always white?

- Do steam rollers really roll steam?

- Why isn't there a tea table?

- Have you ever talked into an acoustic modem?

- Why don't healthy cereals have free prizes in them?

- When the clock was first invented, how did they know what time to set it at?

- Why is it that no plastic bag will open from the end on your first try?

- If a mirror reverses right and left, why doesn't it reverse up and down?

- Why do the signs that say "Slow Children" have a picture of a running child?

- If tin whistles are made out of tin, what are fog horns made out of?

- Why do they call the piece of wood a two-by-four if it's only 1 ¾" X 3 ½"?

- If you melt dry ice, can you take a bath without getting wet?

- Why are there no size "B" batteries?

- If a food processor slices and dices food, what does a word processor do?

- Why do we have hot water heaters?

- What happens to an 18 hour bra after 18 hours?
- Why isn't there a cordless extension cord?
- What would happen if you put a humidifier and dehumidifier in the same room?
- How do you know when you've run out of invisible ink?
- How do they get the non-stick coating to stick on pots and pans?
- Why are hotel showerheads so low?
- Why aren't all the pages in magazines numbered?
- Why does one wheel on a shopping cart always point a different direction?
- What do you put on your luggage tag if your last name is Samsonite?
- How do you sell "No Soliciting" signs?
- Why is it that when you see a shoe in the garbage or street, there's only one?
- Why are fitting rooms so small?
- How do you let someone know you just painted a wet paint sign?
- Why is there a "Wrong Way" sign? How does anyone else know where you are going?
- Why is there no grandchild clock?
- Does anyone ever use the lettered tabs on dictionaries?

- When you open a new bag of cotton balls, is the top one meant to be thrown away?
- What would a chair look like if your knees bent the other way?
- Why is it that an alarm clock goes off by going on?
- Does anyone ever use the mute button on their phone?
- Why are greenhouses not green?
- If you put a coffee mug up to your ear, would you hear coffee brewing?
- Why isn't there a decaffeinated coffee table?
- What's the difference between a couch and a sofa?
- Why is shampoo clear but conditioners are not?
- What's the difference between trash and garbage?
- Why are they called throw pillows and rugs when they just lay around?
- What's the difference between a shrub, a hedge, and a bush?
- Are there any unguided missiles?
- Why aren't there parachutes under plane seats?
- How big does a house have to be before it is called a mansion?
- Why is there no Q or Z on a telephone?
- How do you throw away a garbage can?

Here's another book with Robert Bimler's wit and wisdom, co-authored with his father, Richard Bimler.

This is not a joke book. It's a resource that seriously encourages you to focus first of all on the fact that God loves us and frees us to be his celebrating people in our daily lives – with laughter and good humor.

Let there be laughter in Christ Jesus.

"It is full of practical wisdom to help you and your family live a more joyful, fun-filled, and celebrative life." **Cal Samra, President, Fellowship of Merry Christians**

"The Bimlers call readers to childlike wonder at what the Lord has done and reminds us that for those of us who receive him each day is a day in eternity." **Dr. Jean Garton, National Director of Women of Hope**

To read sample chapters or purchase copies of Laughter! visit www.laughter.2truth.com.

About The Author

Robert Bimler is a 1986 graduate of Valparaiso University, Valparaiso, Indiana. He lives in Seward, Nebraska with wife Rebecca and daughter Abigail. They are members of St. John Lutheran Church. He enjoys celebrating life to the fullest with family and friends!

To purchase additional copies of "Animal Crackers" for yourself, family members, neighbors, friends or enemies, please visit:

www.lulu.com/content/4080961

Thank you for your support!

Reviews

"I praise God...at the same time asking "WHY?"...for the wit and humor of Bob Bimler. What earthly purpose do the answers to these ridiculous questions serve in the great scheme of things? And...I suppose that is exactly the point. We are struggling to make sense of a culture that defines measures and values itself by its ability to answer tough and not so tough questions. Yet, the mystery of our lives and language, and the language of our God's love for us questioning souls, is exactly the "stuff" that makes life vibrant, joyful, and worth living. So ask away, Robert, and incidentally, what do I get if I can actually answer even one of these queries???"

John D. Eckrich, M.D., Executive Director of Grace Place Retreat Ministries

"*Do Vegetarians Eat Animal Crackers?* raises provocative questions with a twist of humor. Not only do the questions that Bimler pose give you reason to pause, they give you reason to laugh out loud. Plus, there's always a gem that you can drop in a social setting or to start a serious discussion. I highly recommend it as food for thought and outright laughter."

Dr. Kurt Senske, President & CEO, Lutheran Social Services, Author, Executive Values: A Christian Approach To Organizational Leadership